No. Wait.
I Can Explain.

Brad Rose

No. Wait. I Can Explain. by Brad Rose
ISBN: 978-1-949790-70-2
eISBN: 978-1-949790-71-9

For information:
Pelekinesis, 112 Harvard Ave #65, Claremont, CA 91711
USA

Library of Congress Cataloging-in-Publication Data

Names: Rose, Brad, 1952- author.
Title: No. wait. I can explain. / Brad Rose.
Description: Claremont, CA : Pelekinesis, 2022. | Summary: "The peculiar
    speakers of "No. Wait. I Can Explain." take liberties with standard
    colloquial speech, invent unusual similes, and employ unconventional
    variants of American idioms in order to offer quirky insights and
    unexpected moments of wisdom about the vagaries of contemporary American
    life"-- Provided by publisher.
Identifiers: LCCN 2022027432 (print) | LCCN 2022027433 (ebook) | ISBN
    9781949790702 (paperback) | ISBN 9781949790719 (ebook)
Subjects: LCGFT: Poetry. | Flash fiction.
Classification: LCC PS3618.O782834 N6 2022 (print) | LCC PS3618.O782834
    (ebook) | DDC 818/.5409--dc23/eng/20220613
LC record available at https://lccn.loc.gov/2022027432
LC ebook record available at https://lccn.loc.gov/2022027433

www.pelekinesis.com

No. Wait. I Can Explain.

Brad Rose

for

Linda and Hannah

"Any fool can cry 'wolf.' To cry 'sheep' is inspired."

Donald Barthelme

CONTENTS

Acknowledgments

Grateful acknowledgment is made to the editors of the journals and anthologies who first published some of the poems contained in this book, earlier versions of which appeared in:

Abandon Journal, "Electric Eels," "Finishing School," and "Teeth"

The American Journal of Poetry, "Uncle Jay," "Bone Saw," "Venom," "Dinner Party," "Like an Accident," "Long Black Car," "Two-thirds of Americans," "Just the Kind of Guy I Am," "Who You Are," and "About the Weather"

Bending Genres, "Baked Alaska," "Last Time," "If the Shoe Fits" and "A Real Catch"

Best Microfiction 2019, "Desert Motel"

Cloudbank, "Climate or Weather?"

Cultural Weekly, "Know Thyself," "Fire Prevention" and "How Do You Do, Mr. Snake"

Fatal Flaw, "Variety" (Best of the Net Nomination and *Best Small Fictions 2022* Nomination)

Feral: A Journal of Poetry and Art, "You're Bound to be in Trouble, But Not for Long"

Flash Boulevard, "Smitten"

Hole in the Head Review, "Who Could Ask for More"

Into the Void, "Land of the Free," "Pets," and "What's the Worst that Could Happen?"

MacQueen's Quinterly, "Keeping an Eye on You" and "Gold Doubloons"

Midwest Review, "Better Mileage"

Miracle Monocle, "Redecorating" and "The Perfect Gift"

Mutiny! Magazine, "What is Known about Gambling"

New York Quarterly, "Apostate"

Nixes Mate Review, "Climate Change"

Prometheus Dreaming, "Not Too Close" (Pushcart Prize Nomination)

Right Hand Pointing, "A Disappearance," "A Perfect Match," "Jackpot," "What I Loved About You," and "Outfit"

Sequestrum, "Suburban Landscape (with Flying Saucer)," "My People" "Rucksack," "Making Money in Today's Market," "It'll be Great," and "A Blast"

Six Sentences, "Hitman Visits the Brooklyn Botanical Garden," "Me and Mrs. X," "Stolen Bikinis," "What I Learned from Hemingway," and "Jack's New Leg"

Sonic Boom, "Taste"

streetcake, "Windows" and "What are Friends For?"

The 45th Parallel, "A Lover's Heart"

Third Wednesday, "Lucky Bullets"

Unbroken Journal, "Land of the Free" "Disguise," "Scooter and Sweet Thing," "Just Like Old Times," and "Insect"

Wild Gods (New Rivers Press, 2021), "Fate"

FATE

I've forgotten my past lives. Like a blind, black dog wandering a night highway, I'm making the best of it.

Without its water, a sea is a desert. Even bad dreams can answer good questions. I never let a disaster go to waste. A river of voltage flows through me, whatever happens, happens for a reason.

Each time I aim with my eyes closed, I hit the bullseye. I make it look like an accident.

DESERT MOTEL

Today is fever bright, no wind. Justine says I should slow down, but I speed up. I like to get to things before they get to me. She's been searching for her birth mother. It's taken her about two years to get this far. I tell her she probably won't recognize her. She laughs and says, *Curtis, not every day has to be a maybe.* Everybody wants something real. When we get to Vegas, she opens her purse and pulls out a birth certificate. It's a single page, and on the back, it has tiny ink footprints and a large thumbprint. The motel is pink and white, and our room is cold as a skating rink. I sit on the end of one of the twin beds, drinking a Cherry Coke. Outside, it's 102 in the shade. The pool is filled with screaming kids. You can hear them having fun, or something like it. I remind Justine there are more plastic flamingos in the world than real ones.

About the Weather

It's natural disaster season, so I start screaming at the fish. Maybe I should be yelling at the bait, but like most people, I can't pay attention to more than one thing at a time. Are my dreams about the future or the past?

Everything seems backward when you sleep in reverse.

For years now, geographers have measured acres and acres of paragraphs. Some of them, they tell us, may even be fertile. Yesterday, I caught my food meditating again— and this time, not just the vegetables. Now, I'm slinking low and smooth, like an octopus gliding through an ocean of gasoline.

I'd like to eavesdrop on myself, just to be on the safe side, but you know how things have a tendency to go bad if you let them. Like Edward Smith, Captain of the Titanic, said just before setting sail, *Even if you carry an umbrella in the Sahara, you can never be too careful when it comes to rain.*

Two-thirds of Americans

Two-thirds of Americans believe their intelligence is above average. I'm their exact same height. Evidently, water doesn't know when it's boiling. Last summer, when we checked in to the Asteroid Motel, the pool water started swimming uphill. It was cool. After some frantic up-selling, Florine said our trip might even be tax deductible. She's a retail genius. How far back does the past go? One day, we drove out of town, past the little factories spread out in their horizontal gravity. They were accessorized by smoke. Of course, I can't tell you where we buried the gold. On our drive back into town, Florine said that overhead, on the old railway bridge, she saw a teenage girl, dressed in black, holding a gun to her head. I told her the only thing I remember about Joan of Arc are the flames.

PETS

Science has shown that you shouldn't name your livestock if, one day, you intend to eat them. I bend easily to temptation, especially when I'm landlocked by energy fields.

Normally, I do all my own thinking, but sometimes I hear things in my sleep. I don't care what the Constitution says, the guilty aren't innocent until proven guilty. Some people think the roses are beautiful at this time of year. Regrettably, I don't own dessert plates.

Yesterday, I gave my notice at work. They wanted to make everyone a cost center, but at my salary, who can afford that? My sister tells me you can make a lot of money in the edutainment industry, but what good is it if the dead are miserable and unwilling to learn? Maybe it's just a phase? Say, you look like you could use a break. Come on in. Be sure to close the door behind you. No. Don't pet him. He bites.

FIRE PREVENTION

Once, I fell asleep in a fire. It was OK. I'm inflammable. Marguerite says that, like eleven fingers, I have an unusual condition. Sometimes, I talk backwards to the bathroom mirror. Like igniting a kerosene blaze with a rain-damp match, what's hard for some is easier for others. Just when you think you've got your chemicals perfectly mixed, you begin to hear voices in your head again. Mine are whispers about sparks. Yesterday, Marguerite texted me. She said, *Don't forget, you're out on your own recognizance.* Later, as I was carrying my gas can up Lake St., the police stopped me. I told them, *I look a lot like my identical twin.* They didn't crack a smile, but they let me go. I went home and locked myself in. Eventually, every fire burns itself out. I felt much better after I listened to the flames.

Uncle Jay

I used to skydive as the crow flies. I didn't want to admit it, but then, the anesthesia wore off. Now, the faster I travel, the slower time passes. One minute follows another, but not in that order.

A dead barber cuts no hair. Maybe it's some kind of strange sex thing?

Yesterday, I ran all the red lights. It gave my car something to do. I felt bad that I didn't feel worse, but I think my brain may be changing. Stop-and-go sleep or just lawless mindlessness? Why would anyone want to hit the brakes? A hundred years from now, it will be a century later. You just can't stop the future.

When I was a kid, we moved around a lot. We weren't poor, just tormented. Uncle Jay used to tell me he kept a spare pair of pants in his car, in case he had to leave, suddenly. He looked like he was waiting to be struck by lightning. Once, the police caught him while he was robbing a dress store. *Wait a minute*, he yelled, *I can't seem to zip this thing up.*

Apostate

I'm proportionally accurate. I don't care if God has a plan. It's for aesthetic effect. Since the sky had its roof blown off, nobody knows what to make of my dreams. In absentia, I'm rehearsing my stage presence. I've only got two degrees of separation.

Yesterday, I tried speaking in longer sentences, but I was cut short. Fortunately, I wasn't born yesterday. They say everything is relative. Last week, I heard God say, *Why does anyone deserve a life that's better than anyone else's?*

Of course, it's not unusual for the violent crime rate to spike over the weekend. If you're only a soldier, you must appear to be an army. Like a mosquito drowning in tomato juice, I feel cheated. When He spoke to me again, He said, *If you want to hit something, play the drums.*

WHAT'S THE WORST THAT COULD HAPPEN?

The weatherman is predicting either light rain or low flying vultures. Liars can't be choosers. Thanks to my esprit de corps, I'm wearing wall-to-wall bumper stickers, so as soon as I fell a few more trees, I'm going to sleep in late. And why not? My mother says that when they made me, they scraped away the mold.

Someday, I'd like donate all my age-appropriate organs to those in need. Maybe Tuesday or Wednesday. If it hadn't been for that meat cleaver incident at the orphanage, everything would have turned out as planned. Damn those redundant children. When we get home, I hope we at least have enough time for one more fire. It would be a shame to waste all this gasoline.

Lucky Bullets

I have skills I don't know I have. An imitation of a lab experiment, I'm wide asleep. Jade says I look like a search party, lost. I tell her I'm crawling closer and closer toward the target. She says my clothes may be an asylum, but my dreams are a bull's eye. Often, I wonder why I am the way I am, but what good is it answering a question with a question? I may be an unknown quantity, but I'm familiar with strangers. Jade says she's been trained to recognize the signs of counter-intelligence. I remind her that there's something about secrets that forces me to confess. The radio reports that when police officers are involved in a killing, frequently they're merely acting in self-defense. It's not the notes you play that matter, it's the notes you leave out. Life's a gamble, but what are the odds? Tonight, only the snipers are lucky.

WHO COULD ASK FOR MORE?

Just tuned-up my flamethrower, otherwise it wouldn't be a fair fight. God knows, it's not easy working in the service sector. Pretty soon, I'm going to reverse my polarities, too. Shake things up a little. Have you ever wondered what's under all those islands? They look like they've lost a lot of weight. If you asked them, they'd probably blame it on someone else. Of course, before the invention of answers, everyone just had questions. Mostly, they talked to themselves. I'm not complaining, mind you. I mean, who doesn't like a department store holiday? Summer breezes, grass skirts, the hula, no criminal charges pending. By the way, the animals are looking out for something upright and furless that might shoot and eat them. Close your eyes. So many great memories.

At the Crossing

Can't tell whether those are mountains in the distance, or unexploded volcanoes. Let's give them the benefit of the doubt. I'm not sure what's causing this janky weather, but the wind's been in hiding for so long, I heard the swim team's flash mob has been rescheduled until after the flood.

As soon as I can, I'm going to line up, single-file, and cut out the middle man. It's bound to be a once-in-a-lifetime chance to inventory the known unknowns and the unknown unknowns. Of course, during daylight savings time, nothing much happens that can't be explained by dark matter, so I'm thinking about changing religions and moving next door to that drive-through tattoo parlor, you know, *Squiggles*, the one next to the abandoned brain bank. Besides, who can blame me for not wanting to get behind the wheel of a school bus too soon?

It was so dark and stormy that night, and the kids were screaming so loudly, the train whistle barely woke me up in time.

TEETH

I lost my prescription—so I swallowed myself. Am I at a standstill or a dead end? I like to work hard whenever the task is easy.

Once upon a time, I dreamed I'd read a book before it was written. Now, like a one-sided coin, I have no chance. Yesterday, I woke up early. Maybe, I should have slept in?

When I learned that those school children drowned at Shipwreck beach, I lost my appetite. *What a shame*, I thought. *Such pretty little teeth.*

Baked Alaska

Febrile as baked Alaska, I've grown over-heated from tilling the magnetic fields. Of course, I don't expect the dead to remember me. I don't tan, I grey.

Look, you can listen to all the confetti music you want, but to the illicit organ trade, it's all just blood under the bridge. What would be the perfect temperature in Hell, anyway? I told Roxie, *But I like knives,* and she said, *Nobody can be certain whether life is a comedy or a sluggish suicide.*

A mid-sized sedan pulled up. No one appeared to be driving its shiny black hull. All my cells began swimming in little circles, orbiting an empire of fear, and I thought, *They'll never prove we killed her husband.* Just then, limp as a rubber dagger, a newspaper blew by in the hilarious breeze. The trees were kind enough not to laugh.

Just Like Old Times

Tuesday and Wednesday, I experimented on myself. Now, no more cuboid thoughts and I'm sleeping faster than ever. Thanks to the molecule splitters, I just had to replace the blood on the left side of my body, so it only took half the time. Sure, it was expensive, but you can make monthly payments. Of course, whenever anyone asks me how I am, I plead the 5th amendment, but I told Loretta it was those damned UFOs again, so at least I've got that covered. Now I'm receiving the signals much more clearly. They come in smooth and well-groomed. And I don't black out any more; not like I used to. Best of all, the military junta and those explosions at the toy factory now make complete sense. In fact, if I keep my frequency low and don't pay any attention to the internet, it's almost like nothing happened at all.

SWEET THING AND SCOOTER

Like a circus clown at an action-packed funeral, I struggle to put on my selfie mask. All morning, I've been trying to trick the algorithms into playing something a little less swashbuckling, a little more humane—like Gollywog's Cakewalk. Naturally, the Artificial Intelligence would like to think like everybody else, but it's become all too human to make that kind of mistake. Yesterday, as Sweet Thing chased me around the robot nursery, trying to baby talk me to death, I made plans to flee the scene of our too-cute crime. As I donned a pair of avocado-green velour sweatpants and tightened-up my fright wig, I yelled, *We've got enough tchotchkes around here to fill a Hello Kitty toy factory.* Sweet Thing yelled back, *No matter what they say, Scooter, your clothes are lying to you.* What you see is what you get. When I turn up the music, all I get is noise.

How Do You Do, Mr. Snake?

In less than 100 million years, Saturn will lose its rings. You're going to love it, although I have no idea what an ice breaker breaks when there's no ice.

Say, what day of the week do you suppose it is in hell? Everybody's been so busy kissing themselves, my lips are chapped. Of course, it's not a crime to enjoy yourself every once in a while. Now that it's the weekend, the dead are off the clock, so they're sleeping late. And who can blame them? They're beside themselves with excitement.

Meanwhile, back at the clubhouse, I'm doing disguised impressions of myself. Sometimes you've just got to fool yourself into thinking you're not somebody else. At my birthday party, my next of kin, Little Knuckles, said torture is most enjoyed when it's least remembered. Then an angry Serpent jumped out of the cake and barked, *Bring me diamonds more beautiful than God.* It was a lovely day. The sun shone bright and the trees relaxed in the casual breeze. I was more polite than usual to the animals.

CHARRED

Trying to simplify my life, so I threw out all my bills and re-financed my sweater. I may be susceptible to disinformation, but I'm not prone to conspiratorial thinking. Like any red-blooded American mammal, I'm just trying to get my money to grow. Now that the government has banned the wearing of pants, everybody remembers things differently. Thanks to the bad blood between us, nobody in this time zone has the same area code. That's probably why they tore down the old bowling alley right after those lazy pinheads went out on strike. What did they expect? Easy street?

Yesterday, during the thunderstorm, I nearly fell into that old storm drain, the one near Stubby's. It wasn't my fault I wasn't paying any attention. The lightning set a couple of cows on fire, and Billy was jabbering about the invention of barbeque. I told him, in the old days, everyone just ate raw meat. He shouted, *Look out, Arnold*, but before I knew what was happening—just like that—another one went up in smoke.

Better Mileage

I'm driving in circles, trying to make ends meet. Oh, Ohio, why are you so round and tall? Although I'm wearing polka dot socks, I dress spotlessly. Luanne says it may be a shame and a sin, but I think it's just a sin. There are different schools of thought. In my tell-all memoir, an anonymous reviewer asks for my character to be killed off in the first chapter, but I try to do the best I can, even when I'm on fire. Of course, these days, everything burns faster because of the internet, so whenever I'm in my car, I roll down all the windows and savor the bathtub-clean scent of the gasoline breeze. I love the way the petroleum wind shuffles my hair. When Luanne says I'm just chasing my own tail, I tell her, thanks to spontaneous combustion, I get better mileage than ever before. Come to think of it, maybe I am taking the long way around

Redecorating

Like darkness, a person is composed of what they aren't. This winter, the Beach Boys plan to ice skate, just like they did last summer.

I'm taller whenever I stand next to a crowded mini-bar. I started to feel guilty about this, until I realized that company loves misery. So now, by applying inflammable flame retardants to my rain-soaked fire starters, I'm reducing my carbon footprint. Yesterday, Miki said, again and again, that my name is out of date. *Junior, your name is out of date,* she repeated, as I front-loaded my flame thrower. Of course, the key question is whether you should cannibalize or re-purpose. If, while formulating your conspiracy theories, you generously collaborate with others, you're bound to have greater success, although you'll have to share the spotlight with those selfish bastards. Miki says that when she completes her singing mime lessons and we get a little money scraped together, we should redecorate the music room. Although they're loud, she says, the chairs aren't musical.

Climate or Weather?

Today's temperature will be noisy. I took it up with the subcommittee. Oh, their tenderness. You don't know me and I don't know you, but I'm sure sex won't cure it. Wait, I know the maracas are in here, somewhere. It's a dangerous business.

Science would have us believe the weather will take the world by storm, but I have no idea why Mt. Everest is getting taller.

Thursday, I made a fleeting appearance at the Bureau of Missing Persons. They told me to come back on Saturday, when they'd be closed. I refused to leave my fingerprints as a down payment. Sure, I like to drink in the afternoon, especially somewhere dark and useless. It's great for brain function, although there's no work quite like clockwork. Say, what's this? I don't know for sure, but I'm told a cat has nine of them.

Windows

Wednesday, on the way to the car wash, my car caught fire. And not the good kind, either. Sheila came running up to me and said, *Everything is getting worse and worse.* I told her the main problem is there's no solution. Everything has a life of its own. You keep trying and trying, but no matter how hard you try, before anyone knows you're gone, you're back where you started. Say, what ever happened to What's-His-Name? You know, Mr. It's-on-the-Tip-of-My-Tongue? Yeah, that guy; the one who hardwired the software and debugged the earworms. Before he disappeared, didn't he buy that bogus kidnapping and ransom insurance? I guess these days you can't be too careful. No, don't pay any attention to the venom-colored sunlight. I just painted the windows. They only look like they're snakes.

If the Shoe Fits

I work hard all day, like a snake. My bankruptcy attorney says it's futile to reinvent the hula hoop, but I tell him it's all part of my journey. I mean, why do we get only one life wedged between two eternities? I'm sure there's a perfectly reasonable explanation, although I haven't been asked to sign the guest register, yet. Thankfully, they found that all those anonymous deaths at the census bureau were unrelated to terrorism. I didn't take it personally. I'm sure it's a lot harder than it looks.

Last night, I barely got an ounce of sleep. Those damn rabbits snored louder than a fleet of crop dusters dangling over a buckwheat farm, but what can you expect if you grow nothing but carrots? After the government's scheduled welfare executions, I'm planning to rename myself, just to be on the safe side.

You know what they say: In a violent breeze, the sky is always filthy quiet. Besides, I wouldn't be caught dead wearing my stilts in a Big and Tall store, certainly not before I'd spellchecked my cookie tattoos. Those 3-D food printers are a lot prettier than they taste. Say, you don't think these slippers make me look fat, do you? Ever since the amputations, I can barely get them on.

ONE REASON FOR THE FRENCH REVOLUTION

The Miami real estate market is so hot, it's melting the north Pole. Naturally, you can't tell who's innocent and who's guilty just by looking at a courthouse. My doctor says I'm not taking enough drugs, but I told him that in a flight simulator, a bird doesn't need any wings. Luckily, after my last bank job, I had enough money left over to have my fortune read by Madame Pomade. She took one look at my greasy lifeline and said that if I eat my Spumoni upside down, it won't have any calories. Hey, it's Paris fashion week, again. Yeah, I know what you mean. Don't you just love the emperor's new outfit? I'm telling you, that guy dresses sharper than a guillotine. Some people say he's not wearing much, but in my opinion, he's always dressed to kill.

SAME-DAY DELIVERY

I'm always going somewhere, even when I'm not making deliveries. My friend, Riley, says I should have been born with four wheels, instead of two legs.

Tuesday, the sky got black as a funeral, but I kept on driving. Headed right toward the lightning. They say those forks are hotter than the sun.

I'm working, but it's not like the ads say, in my *spare* time. Mostly it's just go, go, go. You know, *Buy one, get one free.*

Riley says, although I'm not my own boss, at least I'm not sitting behind a desk.

Yesterday, in that downpour, a pickup behind me, slammed on its brakes, spun counterclockwise, then flipped over into the ditch. I didn't have time to stop, too many deliveries. Later, I heard on the news that the kid who was driving was pronounced dead at the scene. Only 26 years old.

I used to wonder what's in all these boxes and packages. Not so much anymore. Every day is different, only for me, now they're all pretty much the same.

ANDROMEDA

Now that I've tuned-up my force field and miniaturized my plasma deflector, I'm not as anxious as I used to be about Andromeda hurtling at 70 miles per second toward the Milky Way. Of course, it's no longer business as usual. This season, I'll be selling my sweaters to the moths.

I spent all day yesterday trying to make some honest mistakes, but wouldn't you know it, those beige parrots swooped in, like it was a sign of something colorful. Last night, Uncle Billy said, *Don't get too smart for your own britches. Remember, Jesus didn't need a bible.* Talk like that makes me wonder what color the Red Sea is, but I've got a feeling that ladder doesn't have any rungs. After a little hemming & hawing, to-ing & fro-ing, automatic weapon fire erupted in the strange distance. Billy leaned in, his eyes dead as a hit and run, and said, *The devil is made of asbestos, burning, Leon. Know what I'm saying?* I hunkered down, like a hole in the earth, as the stars cinched tighter in an ill-fitting sky.

Genius Lessons

I was just talking to myself and having quite pleasant electrostatic sensations. I always like to make a good first impression. I especially like processing information about information processing. It's easier that way. Whenever I grow tired of my experience, I re-imagine my skeleton, the way a butcher dreams of missing fingers. Naturally, there's only so much you can accomplish in 24 hours. Since the freak accident at the power plant, my receptor synapses have been firing faster than ever, although it's probably better for the both of us that you don't stand too close to me. Of course, you never know when you've prophesized enough self-fulfilling prophesies to become smarter than yourself, so I've been taking weekly, half-hour genius lessons. I'm a quick study. As you can see, lightning has already taught me everything I need to know about electrocutions.

WHO YOU ARE

Yesterday, while my avatar was exercising incognito, I had an epiphany in Esperanto. Of course, whenever it rains, a good roofer is hard to find. In a separate compartment, I ordered the deluxe junior— just in case the extra-medium small doesn't fit. You know how you often want things before you know what they are? That's why I like to say everything twice, especially in my sleep. In fact, before making a phone call, I rehearse what I'm going to say, so the call will go swimmingly the first time.

Because I've got a pool in my backyard, some people think I've got it made. Its blue water, smooth as a snake, permanently faces the open mouth of the sky. Yesterday, I overheard Mr. A. say to Mr. B. *I hate my anonymity.* Then, from behind his disguise, Mr. B. said, *And I hate my impersonality.* It's not who you are that matters; it's who you aren't. I wonder why my attorney always carries a gun?

Jackpot

That's one scary elevator. At least no one was crushed twice. No, no, nothing serious. She was just a clown friend of mine. Eventually, she'll be remembered fondly. Personally, I try to remain in the vicinity of my organs. One time, she was teaching me the right way to be a criminal, and I misheard her. I thought she'd said mutually assured *seduction*. But I didn't let that come between us. We nearly got away, too. Anyway, most of the time nothing happens around here. Nil, zilch, nada. Three-hundred-sixty-five days a year. Three hundred sixty-six—if you hit the jackpot.

ELECTRIC EELS

Millions of Americans have been affected by identity theft. It's probably the greenhouse gasses. Remember that time I voted for the opposition robots? On election night, the intergalactic aliens called and complained. I hope they don't hold a grudge. Now, I'm lying low— quiet as a bottom-feeding catfish—although sometimes, I just can't help myself, I feel as animated as Dr. Frankenstein at the prospect of a thunderstorm. My electrician says life is one, long, low-voltage electrocution, until your bill comes due. Then, everyone gets capital punishment. When I tell him all good things must come to an end, he says, *No one enjoys being hit by lightning, Buster. Except the eels*

LAST TIME

Friday, before the cocktail hour, I went shopping for loopholes. Bridget said it's been her life-long dream to own one. Downtown, I felt like an animal lost in an animal city. So many attorneys. Fortunately, I was my other self, so I was able to take full advantage of my tricky symptoms. Of course, I've never been a big fan, but my reputation preceded me. As is often the case with heroes, it was said about me, *We can't say enough about him.*

No use flying off the handle, especially at gratuitous compliments. Who am I to accuse others of making false accusations? Transitions, like homicides, are always so difficult. Little Monte wouldn't let me get away with murder. *There aren't enough bodies to go around*, he said, although, if the truth be told, I nearly dropped a bomb on myself. But that was before I realized, sooner or later, something has to kill you. Like Oedipus said, if you can't beat them, join them, particularly if you're not sure whose side you're on.

I made the strongest case I could make against cannibalism. No way I'm going to get pink-eye. Not like I did last time.

You're Bound to Be in Trouble, But Not for Long

Now that the Supreme Court is using X-Rays to decide who's innocent and who's guilty, why should I go all to pieces when I'm hit by lightning? I've seen worse. I grew up in Hell's Kitchenette. Yesterday, around noon I was sipping some toy wine and thinking I should talk to my personal injury attorney, but he'd stolen the horses, and lit out for the dormitories. Like choosing between a striped dress shirt and a checked pantsuit, it felt like a prisoner's dilemma. Thank goodness it's still a free country. Of course, it's not every day you get a chance to lock your family in the family room. Juniper says I sure know how to have a good time, even though I'm strictly DIY and do all my own sleepwalking. Fortunately, I'm not religious, because I'm a big supporter of interstellar nepotism, although I receive some bad information every now and then. You know what they say: opportunity knocks when you're least prepared. Say, what are you planning to do with the body of that little green man? It's not even close to dinner time yet.

THE SECOND LAW OF THERMODYNAMICS

The fiscal valley is a model gesture. Dodging a southern synthesis, the continent prevails. In particular, the larger valleys commission an egregious tragedy, but as luck would have it, feedback simulates a wound without which, only a broken heart is well-suited to tell the tale. There are no flashing coordinates, no acute angles. Loopholes are strictly forbidden. Years pass before danger permeates the respectable countryside.

At first, the populace seems distracted by an intimate breeze and its impending nocturnal zoom, then, like milk spilling from a broken oyster, awful cheating begins to fashion its own silhouette. The ruthless strategy soon takes its deadly toll, as the mature bodies of the populace sink below the rescue, and the ensuing riots resemble bread. Although no horizon disappears without its own demeanor, the assistive confluence is undeniable.

Baffled, politicians inaugurate musical scales, diagnoses are outlawed, and the military incentivizes truncated yawns. Even funerals are dismissed. But to no avail. Surveying the landscape's mayhem, astronomers conclude the wreckage was not just unavoidable, but highly permissible. The hours rot whatever preceded misfortune. Someday, perhaps, historians will write of the telltale signs of sloppy petroglyphs and the pitfalls of bungled omniscience. Archeologists will uncover the ancient candy of the guilty. Science may even shed its specious glow. Until then, however, we must rest assured in the knowledge that not since the beginning of time, has time escaped the dogma of the anecdote, the gratified smirk of the repeat offender, nor certainly, the second law of thermodynamics.

Bone Saw

A few minutes after we pass the whirling white blades of the wind farm, I hear a thump, dull and solid, under the front wheels. Roberta flinches, and asks, *Did we hit something?* but just like when I'm drinking alone, I don't say anything, and drive on. As the hollow clouds sprawl across a blue, ceaseless sky, I think, *Animals have souls, too.* A few more miles, the silence between us empty as the Mojave, and she says, *Sometimes, my skin feels like it's inside-out.* I still don't say anything, but I know what she means. Since her husband's "disappearance," I've felt like my bones have been crawling sideways, away from heaven. Roberta turns to me and asks, *Darrel, don't you think that sooner or later somebody's going to find out?* I haven't told her yet about the extent of the damage; it'll be weeks before they finally find and reassemble all his missing pieces. By then, we'll be deep into Mexico, maybe as far as Guatemala. I reassure her, *Don't worry baby. That creep will never hit you, or anybody else, again.*

NEW CLIENTS

Just to be on the safe side, God prays to himself. That way, everybody's a winner. Of course, even with the safest surgery, there can be unexpected complications. It's hard to tell if it's due to organized crime or organized religion.

Sometimes, I'm on a different frequency spectrum. Like ants at a picnic, I'm all over the place. Yesterday, I was innocently piloting my new drone above the neighbor's backyard—just wanted to give it a quick once-over— and wouldn't you know it, the twins were lounging naked again, except for their sidearms.

Sure enough, there was some inadvertent gunfire, so I said to Psycho Kitty, my assistant and lucky charm, *Have you noticed how, lately, the suburbs have become such a concrete jungle?* Kitty snarled, *I don't think the twins are a gang, Terry. They look more like a cult.*

The average person gets only so many winning lottery tickets in a lifetime. Today, I'm feeling lucky as a bulldozer in a China shop. Do you suppose God's accountant is accepting new clients?

Keeping an Eye on You

After watching edible television, I'm learning to talk to myself. *Thinking* means different things to different people. Consider the spaghetti western. Simple living requires getting rid of things that you don't enjoy or that will kill you. Even on summer days the sun keeps its distance. No use getting all riled up.

In case I have to rename myself, I'm going to assume a mistaken identity. Can't wait to see the sequel. Yesterday, I took a walk in the park and realized I am the garden. Sometimes my brain gets on my nerves. When it does, I lip-sync until I align with my pseudonyms.

If you see something, say something.

I don't want to watch you sleep at night, but I do.

TWISTER SEASON

I was trying to levitate myself again. Without a license. They say you shouldn't do it without a license. At least I waited until after the holidays. LuAnn nearly hit the ceiling when I told her. Billy assured her it was alright because I hadn't had a drink in nearly two days. Billy also mentioned that I hadn't exceed 60,000 volts, so normally, there would have been no worries. Of course, neither of us expected a house fire to break out right in the middle of an earthquake. No one likes to upset LuAnn, needlessly. Not with twister season coming on.

Suburban Landscape (with Flying Saucer)

In the Great Big Picture Book of Lies my picture doesn't look like me. Recovering from a Lego injury, I'm wearing my mild socks. Mine is not a smile, but a simper. I'm not pushing the envelope, I'm an actor played by a husband. Sure, the kids are sober and the chimney has stopped smoking, but I look like an estranged taxidermist working remotely from a rental doomsday bunker in the Catskills.

Clarise is mad at me, as usual. The car won't start. The house plants have died on my watch. The cat, emulating the parrot, imitating the dog, has begun barking. Sitting in the back yard now, as far away from the unpaid bills as is humanly possible to be and still reside at this address, I'm wondering if Michelangelo had had a dog, would he, Michelangelo, that is, have painted the Sistine Chapel or settled for linoleum? I have a life-long student debt, whose associated student escapades have placed me on the fast-track, in slow motion. I think we have termites. At night I can hear them chewing. The roof leaks when it's not raining. The washing machine refuses to rinse. Last week, I heard about a UFO crash on the edge of town. The mayor assures us it's nothing serious, but what does he know about interstellar debris? There are no signs of intelligent life in his administration. The museum closed, the schools are sub-par, the sub-flooring is optimal, and the overhead is killing me. Yesterday, when Jack came over, I hardly recognized his car, it was so clean. Ours is a moon vehicle covered in both brown dust and red rust— the earthy colors of an alien planet. Janine wants horseback riding lessons. She thinks *Equestrian* will look good on her college applications. Her sister is studying internet dating.

BRAD ROSE

I hate the neighbors, except for Michelle, the cute one, hemmed in on our cul de sac. She smiles at me like I'm not married. If I were to be fired from my current management-manqué job, it would be a celebratory disaster. I'm reading about how to become a change agent in a cashless economy. I'm afraid I'm coming up short. My pajamas are floral hexagons in a brilliant shade of jungle puce. When I drink, I see wires. I'm dieting exclusively on chocolate cake.

Yes, we have roses growing along our white picket fence, but I don't understand the transmigration of souls. When the police arrive, I assure them I was nowhere near the scene of the crash, but inform them that ever since, Clarise has been acting a little funny. With his tentacle-like hand on his holstered firearm, the younger cop—the one whose face is slightly inhuman—tells me to put my hands over my head and that he knows the name of a good lawyer. It's his brother. He's new in town, he tells me, and doesn't yet have any reputation, to speak of.

LEOPARD PRINT

Spent all month cutting and pasting. After a while, like the alphabet, you get used to it. Of course, you can't help but wonder, *Who are all these blue-eyed animals?* even on horse day. Fortunately, all my muscles are connected. Magnolia assured me that everything looks better in leopard print. That's why whenever I'm given a choice, I like to choose the house that isn't burning.

A Lover's Heart

Louanne threw an *x* on me, so now, I'm only able to do the ugly dance. I like to put everything I say in quotation marks because it makes me look smarter. My astrologer says I should keep my cutting edge sharpened and everything will work out fine. As usual, I'm spreading the positivity, because everything feels better with Novocaine.

Tuesday, I was walking through the old neighborhood and doing my machete math when I thought, *I need a slogan.* Something like, *It's entirely painless, except for the pain.*

Something has got to be done about those damn inflammable molecules. I mean, what are the chances of sleeping in a fireproof room? Louanne assures me that in a house fire, every room burns at room temperature. Three haircuts later, and I finally understand why Cupid said it's only true love, if the arrow leaves a serrated hole in your heart. Fortunately, *forever* is only one lifetime long. *X* marks the spot.

What I Learned from Hemingway

I'm an oenophile, so I'm not afraid of bulls. Wednesday, I realized that if I lose a limb, it probably won't grow back. *And not a minute too soon*, Lady Charise said. *Those animals are fast. Do you think it's the caffeine?* I have, of course, kissed other girls.

JUST GIVE IT A PUSH

My lawn left town, that liar. Then the government launched a crackdown on the government.

Like that isn't the oldest trick in the book.

Last year, I had a nervous break-up. Now, thanks to the Secret Adjective Society, everybody's romance is getting modified. So far there's been no evidence of atrocities, but we're only half-way through the fiscal year. Murphy says that because of the law of contradiction, I'm the smart kind of stupid. I want it both ways. I told him you only have to be two things in life and death. Both of them are lucky.

Of course, I'm not saying it's illegal just because of the boisterous entrails. I'm just saying never use your real name, unless you're willing to wear your big-boy dinosaur pants. But enough of all this divine light; let's get this goddamned thing going, shall we?

The Larches

Great question. Yeah, I like the alphabet just as much as the next person. What you see is what you get. Of course, a pirate is just a flamboyant thief. It makes you wonder if God is an atheist. Say, did you see those holes punched in the nearest lobe of heaven? I wish the trees would stop their fighting. When they're not throwing punches around, they have such lovely personalities, especially the larches. I hope there are no hard feelings.

Love is Like That

I'm my own outfit planner. McKenzie says I look like I'm waiting for an execution. She says my clothes may increase my risk of infection. Both my shoes and my feet are asleep.

Generally speaking, I like medium-sized objects, but there are always exceptions. Sure, there may be life on other planets, even the Disney planets, but there's no accounting for taste. I don't remember my passwords, the same way some people don't want to be found.

Not sure if I'm using a pseudonym or a nom de plume, but just in case, I've got a pair of those little black x-ray sunglasses—you know, the kind for watching an atomic bomb explode. McKenzie says it could occur at any moment, and if it does, it won't be a minute too soon. I tell her, *It's never too late to pretend like nothing happened.* Love, if you let it in, is exactly like that.

Venom

I was trying to confuse the algorithms by de-calibrating my snake detector, but wouldn't you know it, the damn thing was booby trapped. I asked my cosmetic surgeon if she could make me look smarter than my IQ. She immediately made an excuse; said the neighbors were listening. Now the weather lies to me whenever it wants. Of course, to the stereotypical sleep walker, anything can happen. It's the old mind/body problem—nobody's got a skeleton—although I prefer to think of it as a typical freak accident. Sometimes though, the meteors bore through a bored, night sky, their redundant combustion like firefighters using fire to fight fire. Other times, especially when the bees are asleep, it's just bad luck. When I lost my car in last year's flood, did you hear me complaining about climate change? No, of course you didn't.

It's not stealing if you plan to give it back. Those snake bites can be cute as a button, especially before the venom reaches your brain. Too bad no one is looking.

ONE THING I LEARNED FROM JOHN ASHBERY

Look, it's Kierkegaard again, frolicking, as usual, without a hat, in the poppies.

Sure, those boa constrictors are lovely, until you run out of gas, then it's back to putting all your eggs in one basket, at least until all hell squeezes over. Needless to say, acupuncture is needles, so by all means, don't hesitate to be late. No, those homo sapiens aren't fakes, they're copies of themselves, even if they look like cardboard cutouts made from human beings. They're really authentic. Regrettably, it can't be helped.

It'll be Great

This time, you'll have to do the exact same thing as last time, only differently, or it won't come out the same. It's because of the unintended consequences. The left hand doesn't know what the right hand is doing. Fortunately, what happens behind the curtain, stays behind the curtain. It's better that way, especially if you believe it only in your head. Naturally, some people think it's worse at night, because then, you have no one to answer to, and if you do, they hardly ever call you back.

On a positive note, all the glitches and snags are now completely subsidized. You know, *the government.* It's not like last time, when it happened in real time rather than the other kind, and no one was prepared until after it was too late. Absolutely no one. Except for that guy from X-Ray. Yeah, that guy, *Bones.* He claimed he could see through the whole thing, right from the very beginning—even earlier. He said he knew it was going to happen, before it happened. Saw the whole thing coming. Of course, he would say that, wouldn't he? Some people are just that way. There's one in every crowd. They stand out because they blend in. One in a million. Like a sore thumb.

Anyway, I hear this year, it's going to be a short summer. Really short. Just June, July, and August. It'll be over before you know it. Just like that. A split second, and *boom.* Over. It's leap year, you know. Not like all the rest. It has a way of sneaking up on you when you least suspect it. The months fly by, and then just like that, *That's all she wrote. Fini. The End.* I hope this time, it doesn't take too long to get here. Hope it happens so fast your head will spin. Hope it's here and gone before you know it. Over before it's started, and

BRAD ROSE

not a minute too soon. I don't know about you, but I can hardly wait. You'll see. It'll be like nothing you've ever seen. You'll see. As soon as it gets here, it'll be great.

Dinner Party

It's tear gas season and everyone is weeping. They think the dead are unoccupied, but actually they're quite busy. Today, the clouds are drowning in the shallow end of the sky. Some people want to burn their bridges, but I prefer to get my energy from plants and animals.

Although I hate heights, I've never been accused of a bad altitude. I am my own best friend. With a little luck, I'll wake up exactly in the same place where I fell asleep.

Outside, like the approach of war, it grows darker and darker, but it's always daylight-saving time on the bright side of the moon. Of course, meal time occurs at all hours on different planets, but I'm hungry as the Donner party on its last leg. Let's eat.

Like an Accident

Saturday night, I drove out of town, into the desert, so I could count lightning strikes. Like a black balloon splattered with streaks of white paint, the sky stretched and spread until it popped. A couple of forks struck pretty close. On the way back, I stopped at *Cannibal's* for a drink. I love it when I order a Bloody Mary there. Nobody bats an eye. Charlene was there, drinking alone, so I told her about the time they wouldn't let me take my emotional support gator on the plane. She laughed so hard she nearly dropped her darts. *It's the damn government,* she said, as she recovered and hit the bullseye. I said, *Yeah, they're everywhere, but what are you going to do?* I like Charlene. Not sure whether her 4th husband just died or not. I don't think she's available, yet.

If I had a life insurance policy, I'd let it expire. Never liked my next of kin. No sense of humor. Of course, thinking about the end is something everybody should do. It's perfectly natural. When my time comes, I'm going to make it look like an accident.

OUTFIT

Every sentence benefits from a verb. Naturally, this time of year, with everything so seasonal, it can't be prevented, so I like to be lucky, even when nobody is looking. Yesterday, for instance, I was paid in knives. Today won't last as long as yesterday, because now I'm doing things that don't have names, but why stick to my talking points? About half an hour ago, I plummeted into a seething nest of baby rattle snakes. You know how it always seems like there are more of them than there are of you. Hey, did you pick that outfit yourself?

KNOW THYSELF

Pointy and loud, the geese, heading in a southerly direction, bark at a horse-gray sky. Is it any wonder? At breakfast, I apologize to my sunny side-up eggs. Like a bad actor, I give an unforgettable performance. Everyone has grown tired of reading books about books. Like New York, New York, or a forest for the trees, it's just mise en abyme. Fortunately, it's nothing serious.

Sometimes you play your best during rehearsals. Yesterday, for instance, I was just going through the motions, but I had all my ducks in a row. My ornithologist reminded me that beauty is usually only skin deep, and that brain eating isn't the weirdest thing that happens in the animal kingdom. Of course, we know so little of others, and almost nothing at all of ourselves. *Great Tits*! I exclaimed.

LAND OF THE FREE

I'm in the park. I'm light enough to float. My brain is stronger on the right side. What does it matter where my ideas come from? Is there ever only one thing at a time going on in your mind? I can see the latest birds, now. They look like bullets shooting from those trees. Little black bullets jumping into the sky. The clouds are nice; a little shade, if it doesn't rain. Thinking about the angry fish I saw in Chinatown, yesterday. Can't get them out of my head. Orange and yellow—little, ugly, fat cigars.

Sometimes I wish I wasn't single, but I always try to have a good time. Someone, who I shall call Maxine, said, *Isn't it a shame about that subway crash?* She's right. All those people crushed in a smoking, coal-black tunnel. Probably veterans and pregnant women. A *car mishap* the news said. I should write a letter to the editor. An anonymous letter. What's wrong with this country? Whose side are we on, anyway?

HIT IT OUT OF THE PARK

I like music other people are afraid of. They say the robots are going to put me out of my job, but I've still got a steady groove. Sometimes I fall asleep in the rain.

I talk to myself even when I don't want to. Nobody's called the cops yet, not even my ex-fiancé. Of course, I'm not blaming anyone. Yesterday, I drove out of town, on Route 6. Watched the wheat blow in the smooth, clean wind. I don't know why they arrested that Psychic in town. Everyone said she looked like an imposter. I think she struck a nerve when she predicted last summer's bad harvest. Now I'm here at the baseball diamond. It's not really a diamond, it's a square. Anybody can see that. Not sure who's going to win next Saturday's game. The future is hard to tell. I don't know why they call it *Little League*. Once, I had to use a Louisville Slugger on my 6th grade teacher. Bright as blood, the sunlight shone everywhere. That bat didn't look that small to me.

DISGUISE

I stopped at a Mobile mini-mart, and bought some gas and groceries. You can buy hair dye in a mini-mart, change your hair color in the bathroom, if you need to.

Sometimes, I hear the deep blue wire of the sky, hissing. Even at night, when the clouds crawl on their soft knees through the dark.

Bare hands are the windows of the soul. That's what the Bible says.

When Loretta broke up with me, she promised she'd always love me, even if after she turned 14, her daddy made her marry another man. That Loretta, cute as a button.

I hate driving these back roads across the state line. At least I don't have to wear a wig in all this goddamned heat.

A PERFECT MATCH

Sometimes, when God matches dreams with sleepers, he makes terrible mistakes, but if you don't own a driver's license, it can't be revoked. They say motion slows the passage of time, so I'm going to trampoline all night on National Sleep Day.

On the ride over here, the radio reported that multiple fires in the neighborhood appeared suspicious. With a glint in her eye, Kandy reminded me that wherever there's smoke, there's arson. Kandy is a philosophy major. She believes only a fireman can feel at home in a burning house. I realize, of course, not every woman is right for me.

GOLD DOUBLOONS

In a public/pirate partnership, the galleons build themselves. Who's to say if it's smooth sailing? I haven't got my sea legs yet. Too busy adding wow to my overcrowded decluttering agenda. I love merch, so it's hard to know whether I should keep the pins and needles and discard the needles and pins, or vice versa. Like the suspension of disbelief, this week, I'm shadowing myself at work. No, you go on ahead, I'll catch up. To be perfectly honest, over all these seafaring years, I've grown a little lightning-prone. Sure, I've got impressive dance moves, even if being a buccaneer is to regret not having more limbs. Although every pirate must put on his or her britches one leg at a time, Lady Justine says she admires the way I've embraced one-armed hobbies, the kind that can, like fencing, leave me simultaneously single handed and headless. *It doesn't take a genius to walk the plank,* I told her. *You ought to know, Flat Top,* she breezily responded. Shiver me timbers.

THE PERFECT GIFT

Last weekend, on my way to the Brotherhood of Thieves, I counted everything I passed on the street, and before I could tell whether I was high-fiving or swing dancing, I ran out of natural numbers. It's my cranky algorithm. It refuses to cooperate with the data purge.

When I tried to explain to my boss that virtual reality is a fake rumor, he wanted to examine the exculpatory evidence. It's futile to tell the truth to lie detectors.

Last night, I dreamed I woke up to my dream job. There was money everywhere. As I de-linted myself and corrected for my distracted driving, a Norse folk song started to play. I couldn't stop myself from singing along with my own mouth. Who can resist a sexy Viking? Sure, the drum solo was too long, but I'm a bad listener.

Although the price of helium has shot sky high, party balloons are always in the national interest. Like the disappeared corpses of the opposition, they're the perfect gift for any oligarch. Just ask the dead.

WHAT IS KNOWN ABOUT GAMBLING

Even when the roads rage, the sky is still. A fog, I'm everywhere at once, my memories a secret, my nerves like shaved ice. Last night I dreamt of slow thinking, like the green bottom of a winter lake. Days of disbelief, my brain thinks about my brain thinking. Do burning moths appreciate the color of their consuming flames? Juanita says she prefers small game hunting. *And why shouldn't I?* she asks. *Losers love to gamble.* I yield the floor to the ghosts. Although they've paid their dues, even now, they can't get enough.

NOT TOO CLOSE

Me and Nathan-Ray sure worked up an appetite burning all those effigies, but practice makes perfect. On our way back to town, I felt hungry as an empty plate, so we stopped off for some beer and eggs at *The Shed*. We sat at our usual table in the corner, while the busy music jumped like angry canines at the bear-brown walls. Nathan-Ray asked, *Do you think plasma has a hidden agenda, Cole? Can it run uphill like Satan's water?* Nathan-Ray's always thinking about things from the angle of the fire-prevention industry. He's got hard-boiled hair and a trucker's left-sided tan. He swears he never intentionally set anyone on fire. At least not to the best of his knowledge. I told him I didn't know if Satan invented plasma, but I knew for sure that when we drive with the windows rolled down and the empty scrub blurs into a smear of speed, I feel sorry for myself losing all those years in Folsom. Just then, God walked in and took a seat at the counter. He looked dog-tired. He had a long, tangled beard and white splotches of paint dappled all over his cream-white overalls. If you didn't get too close, you could barely see splattered on his clothes and shoes all the mistakes he'd made. The music stopped and the place got quiet as an empty manger. Let's just say me and Nathan-Ray didn't get too close.

Making Money in Today's Market

I was whiteboarding our client-focused, seamless functionalities, prior to holistically leveraging our hyper-scale impact portals, when Jeanine snidely accused Curtis of preemptively facilitating prospective e-business dynamic solutions, although she'd neglected to accurately aggregate her own hyper-monetized, mission-critical, value chain. Personally, I don't like to onboard enterprise-wide synergistic ideas, unless I've front-ended the virtual impactful best-practices, but what are you going to do when two normally user-friendly, colleagues suddenly engage in backend, B2B, click bait malalignments of multi-bandwidth supply chain linkages? So, first, I asked Curtis if he'd cloudified the open-source, cross-platform drivers, or at least future-proofed the cross functional design team fungibility outputs? He gave me a sheepish look and said, *No.* I turned to Jeanine and asked if she'd had a chance to proactively benchmark the optimally aligned, core competencies for 24/7 integrated down-market innovation? She looked gobsmacked. So, then—as much out of resignation as genuine astonishment—I said, *Did either of you even bother to elasticize the next-generation distributed metric leadership modules or de-intermediate the bleeding-edge virtualization infomediaries?* Nada. Zip. Zero. Is it any wonder why low-risk, high-yield, end-to-end, extensible, niche market, top-of-mind visionary entrepreneurs, like myself, aren't able to make a dime in today's clicks-no-bricks, just-in-time, on-demand, bitcoin economy? *OK*, I said, *how much cash do each you have on you? Good. Put it on the table.*

A Disappearance

Like a front porch light left on all day, I have a secret. Without darkness, there is no light. Some people are endlessly curious, most depart without leaving a trace.

I told the motorcycle cop who pulled me over, every particle has an anti-matter twin. Below his white helmet, he smiled like a wasp.

I won't pretend that nothing happened.

Hitman Visits the Brooklyn Botanic Garden

I overhear a teenage girl say to another teenage girl, "I didn't tell Mom we were the ones who killed the cat." The cherry trees are blooming pink bombs. It's early Spring. The day is sunny as an egg. Aimless as a stray bullet, the wind blows past me. I wonder, *Have I chosen the wrong career?*

Jack's New Leg

At our class reunion, no one mentioned it. It would have been cruel, and insensitive. Hoping to avoid any appearance of pity, Marty even refused to help him sit down, although it was clear to everyone gathered, Jack was in lot of pain as he collapsed into his seat. Then Jack said, *And that's not the only thing I lost.* Like machine gun fire, mortified glances shot around the table. War is a lot worse than anyone imagined.

What I Loved About You

Just passed a bowling alley and two liquor stores. Now, I'm thinking of you. Unlike the others, I admired your careless voice, the way the judicial system kept trying to correct you. Like converting an abandoned parking lot to a Zen garden. Smooth grey stones, silent mouths. I recall how you'd say, *Just give me the damn cash.* You were what you were. When I get home, I'll turn on the shower. I love the sound of rain.

COSMOS

What happens to your body when you die in space? I'm only a hypothetical astronaut. Sorry I can't be more cooperative, but at least I'm not redundant again. Only once was I caught wondering about those one-hit wonders. Now, I'm intermittently insouciant—not happy-go-lucky exactly; more quirky than kinky. Needless to say, I've been busy repairing my reputation. So far, no injuries to report, but words only go so far. I wouldn't want to lose my mojo simply because of the square circles everybody has been talking about. They were just discovered. You know, *out there*. I'm telling you, what are we going to do about the cosmos? At the current speed of light, everything is behind the times, so now, I can't tell whether I'm close to the things I'm afraid of, or afraid of the things I'm close to. Fortunately, looking at the Picture of Dorian Grey never grows old. Art may be eternal, but space is really, really big.

Taste

The other day, I was pseudo catastrophizing during an avalanche when, by mistake, I nearly fell off the cliff. Of course, money isn't everything. A lot of things look good on paper, but when you get them home, they try to eat you.

Melissa accuses me, like a dead man, of talking to myself when no one is listening. I told her I'm like that novice magician who tried to cut himself in half. When the police arrived to calm the angry crowd that had gathered to demand a refund, he said: *But my sequined assistant is at home, sick, with the flu.* You'd never find me in a nest of snakes like that. The spider's web knows things the spider can't, but we all want to learn from one another. Because sharks close their eyes as they devour their prey, their teeth help them to learn more about what they're biting. There's no accounting for taste. Even the dead prefer their surgery with general anesthesia.

Yard Sale

I've got a confession to make; I spend too much time with giraffes, but I hate to miss an opportunity to overcome my fear of heights.

Alexander the Great never lost a battle, even in darkness.

Thanks to onomatopoeia I wear my sharkskin houndstooth suit. I love animal haberdashery.

Last weekend, I went to an imposter yard sale. Despite the sign, the yard had been donated to a worthy cause. I have to admit it; I've never seen so many bullet holes in one garage door. Here's to hoping there are no more pet suicides in that neighborhood. I'd like to go back there sometime, when the lightning is brighter.

THE CHERRY TREES INHALE

While the buildings burn, I ignore their brilliant advice. Like the ordinariness of diamonds in a diamond mine, I'm a bystander, but I'm not innocent. The mass of the visible universe is 3×10^{55} kilograms, although it's not very well manicured. Sure, I've got the intangibles going for me, but I'm still worried about what's happening on other planets. It may be none of my business, but the cherry trees inhale more than their share of the sky. Come to think of it, do you swim here often?

What are Friends For?

Those surly gargoyles, their colors are tone deaf. Even if they clean up the space junk, it's probably just a plot device. The globe's richest 1% own half the world's wealth. I guess it's only fair. Have you noticed that my hair's on fire? Sure, I believe fantastic things, but so do you. When I get up tomorrow, I'm going to slip into my flesh bodysuit and listen to some righteous snake music. No, I'm not too worried about death, I'm water proof. Hope it's quick and happens to somebody else, though. Hey, I just forgot everything I said. Pretty sure it wasn't profane and I was using my best church voice. By the way, if I need any help inciting tomorrow's riot, I've got your number. I'll give you a call.

BEE CRAZY

Everybody's crazy about bees. I'm on that list, twice. Palm trees have no wood, provide no shade, and bear little fruit. In Hawaii, what counts as a Hawaiian shirt? My pulse makes a quiet noise, but to be a musician, you must learn to play at least one instrument loudly.

Like invisible sounds in the puppet workshop, I'm uncomfortable in my comfort zone, but if not for its curves, each circle would become a square. Gooch said, *You've got to find something that works the way your brain does,* so, instead of learning to swim, I burned my pajamas. Now, I do only competitive sleeping. It's not as sweet as honey and it gives me hives, but so far—haven't been stung once.

Mr. Lifeguard

Everything happens so carefully, I can barely make an honest mistake, but don't take my word for it; ask my lawyers. Yesterday, Mr. Waters asked me, *At the land fill, whose land are we filling, anyway*? I reminded him not to eat with his mouth full and to avoid the deep end. Sure, I love disembodied partying as much as counting bubbles, but it doesn't matter what color your DNA is; you've got to be in the right place at the right time. Although my weekend visit to the petting zoo threw a monkey wrench into my pool-party plans, I managed to avoid that sinking feeling. I'm optimistic because even when you're on your last legs, you only live once. Of course, I haven't come all this way just to see the light at the end of the tunnel. In fact, since little Kitty's drowning, ours has been the happiest house on the block. No thanks to you, Mr. Lifeguard.

My People

You know, the whole kit and caboodle. Like big, lousy fun. Say, could you pass me that cocktail? I love the little red umbrella. Can you eat the leaves? Yesterday, I felt sad as a birthday party everybody forgot to attend. To make up for it, I bought a book about snakes. The poisonous ones, mainly. I'm reading it out loud. No, no problem, as long as it doesn't wake the dogs. Been listening to a lot of airport dance music, too. Overall, it's pretty invisible, although I hate those gigantic notes. Who are they kidding? Steampunk wasn't invented in the Ice Age.

Remember the time that guy mistakenly shot my cousin, Billy, in the back? Thought Billy was somebody else. And he was. Remember? It happened down at the *Sugar Shack*. In one side and clean out the other. Just missed his heart. Billy was in the hospital for a better part of a year. Nearly the whole town visited him, even my kissy, kissy ex and her big, smiling-sonofabitch-banker husband. Before his accident, Billy sure could drive a semi. Liked long-haul because he liked to be alone whenever he was awake. When I asked him why he still drinks at the *Sugar Shack*, his face got sad and sloppy as a lost bloodhound's, and he said, *Too crowded at the Peanut House.*

How to Survive a Lightning Strike

I'm looking for my long-lost twin so we can compare notes. Sure, I've got a favorite emergency room, but I refuse to attend any more funerals. My parole officer says electricity has a lot of potential, but I'm pretty sure I signed up for a different force field. A lightning bolt is an electrical discharge between the atmosphere and an unsuspecting object. Before he was executed in Texas, my dad said lots of people survive a lightning strike. Next week, I'm going to prepare for the worst. Like a snake bite, it can strike you when you least expect. It's a lot easier to recover than you think. At least for the snake.

INSECT

The police sketch artist says I haven't changed a bit. Like Western civilization since 1500, I'm still not that entertaining, but thanks to my electronic tan, my digital clothes envy me. If you discount their continuous spam, their spark isn't as bad as their light. Sometimes, I see people and they look crisp and clear, like light at the end of tunnel vision, although they tell me I look hazy as Beijing smog during volcano season. I don't know whether it's false consciousness or bad faith, but my eyes are burning and smell like smoke. My ophthalmologist says it's left over from the Big Bang. I hope I haven't missed my window of opportunity.

Aren't you tired of being a seamless visionary of 24/7 transformative cross-platform strategic innovation? I think we should just re-paint the roller coasters and rely on our party verbs. *But where are the ants supposed to bury their dead?* Charlene yells. When I was her age, I was asleep. *Great disguise, Charlene*, I yell back. *Six legs look really good on you.*

Black Box

It's a perfect day to shave my head. Last night was dark as a tar pit and the sheets were so hot, they nearly melted my legs. Nothing is magic, if you know how it's done.

Sometimes, with my butcher knife, I stand in the front yard and twist around like a worm. The passing clouds have no idea what's in store for them. Claudine says that on our street, I laugh the loudest. When I was your age, I blacked out. I got nearly a thousand hits. Now, somewhere else hides inside me, like a jail hides inside a cop's stare. The Museum of Unspeakable Things is close as a whisper. When I get the coordinates, I'd send them to you. If the black box was painted yellow, it would be a lot easier to find after a crash. Of course, the sharpest razor isn't necessarily the truest.

CAREFUL

I've got electricity in my heart, the same as lightning, although I'm a slow listener. There's an ocean in every sea, so what's the use of laughing at a drowning, especially if it's a mermaid's? Underwater, we're all just animals. It requires forgiveness.

Some people say certain parties aren't telling the truth, but every chain needs a weak link. Yesterday, I felt empty as a lawn chair at a yard sale, so I walked around town until I overheard some hearsay. The police sirens explained a lot about local crime. Did you know this is a one-gun-purchase-per-month state? The voters here have no sense of humor. They won't make a mistake like that again. You've got to separate the sheep from the wolves. Just look at what happens when you can't tell which is which.

Of course, some nights are as long as the day is wide, but I never steal anything that doesn't rightfully belong to someone else. I'm careful about things like that. Better safe, than sorry. I like to make a difference in people's lives. I'd hate to break into the same house twice, by mistake.

BRAD ROSE

DEVIL WINGS

This morning, I woke up laughing again, in no uncertain terms. Typically, I dream of hovercraft, but this time, nothing but devil-winged gadgets.

Because I've not been receiving the kinds of e-mail I deserve, I recently joined the clandestine group, Conspiracy Deniers Anonymous. It's a dream come true, although I have an escape plan in case I only receive a suspended sentence. Rusty says the principal problem with a career in fire-setting is all the fires. Time will tell if it's serendipity or merely luck. After our invisible convention, Cosmic Maurice stopped by, and as he dismounted his flying motorcycle, said, *I'll have the orthogonal soup, please.* Even brought his own rectilinear bowl. Cosmo's always prepared for the worst.

Normally, I don't like to ask people for money, so now, while fundraising, I wear only left-handed gloves. I hope it's ok with my support group. They're completely confident our drones will destroy only the enemy's drones. Of course, peace is near and dear to all our hearts, although ever since I can remember, I've tried to forget.

A Real Catch

I'm wearing my lucky pants. Everybody at the post office knows me. Yesterday, when I walking to the liquor store, I noticed somebody peeping through the blinds. I've been trying to trick myself into being invisible, but so far, no luck. For a while, I was thinking about running for office, but since the chainsaw accident, I've been rethinking my electability. Besides, I have my principles.

Lucille says I'm one of her favorites, even if my stomach growls like an old washing machine. She's such a cut-up. I told her the beauty of the beehive is its buzz. I'm my own noise. Too bad Lucille isn't the marrying kind. She's said no to me a million times.

Tomorrow, I'm going to put on my desert camo, and take my dirt bike out to Dry Lake. I like it there because the light is clean and the sand looks like it's asleep. I don't mind if there's no fishing. I never catch anything, anyway.

Embrace Your Fears

No, the dummies were just a random experiment—you know, just hit and miss, mix-and-match—but it's been a real gamechanger. Now, I always buckle my seatbelt twice. I used to think this was a just-in-time economy, but it's really a just-in-case economy.

By the way, it's only human nature to use a square hammer to pound a round nail, especially if you're more average than the average person. Once, I had a winning lottery ticket, but I lost it. Like they say, *C'est la vie, Pokey.* I hope this will be a cautionary tale for children, those wolves, because there'll be no more wearing digital cologne and letting the good times roll for this cybernaut. Of course, it's good to learn what you're up against, whenever you're up against it, especially when you're naked.

There's a thin line between bankruptcy and solvency, so you better be sure you're playing for the right team. What goes around comes around. Sure, it scares me. But, like it or not, I like it.

FLAT EARTH

Saturday, Cal called and said, *You're only cheating yourself if you don't go.* I told him, *No thanks, Bud. What kind of fishing can there be in a place called Empty Lake, anyway?* I hung up, took something for the pain, and lay down, again. Started thinking, I've never gotten anything good in the mail. Then, as I was sinking into the black hole of sleep, my Ex called and said she'd heard that the elderly couple who lived down the street had just been found dead. The cops think it was a murder-suicide. For weeks, the neighbors had heard them screaming at one another in the middle of the night, but on the night of their deaths, no one heard shots. I told her, I don't understand what people think they see in one another. She said, *I know what you mean*, and hung up. The Flat Earth Society has members all over the globe.

NEVER CAN TELL

Every day offers an opportunity to explore your personal style, so yesterday I painted open eyes on my sleep mask. You, too, can learn to see things in a different light. It just takes a little practice.

Sometimes it's hard to know who we really are. Deep down we're all just persons, although those twin robots who received the face transplants at their birthday party are still searching for their birth mothers. This week, thanks to the hollow bees, I received more stings than a flutter of jellyfish. Didn't hurt a bit.

Sure, I've read the Voodoo Bible, but I'm not a member of any clubs. I could care less about the terrorists' rebranding. Melisa says I'm too unfathomable to be deep. What choice do I have? A strict determinist with a mediocre IQ, I always look both ways before crossing the street. As fate would have it, you never can tell.

Good Money

I thought I had sleep paralysis, but it was Martians tying me down again for their experiments. Later, my socks shrunk, but my feet remained the same size. God and the weather; what are you going to do? Tuesday, it was so cold, I turned on the TV. Been following all the procedures to get into heaven. The police department has been very helpful, in that regard. In fact, we're taking it to the next level.

I find almost any recipe is improved by the omission of Spam. The taste is in the pudding, as they say. In sector "K," the code of reality is far-fetched, so it pays to have quirky charm and more fun than an octopus has elbows. Next time, though, I'll have to figure the blood/brain barrier into the final equation. No use throwing good money after bad.

Rucksack

It's a nice, cool night since those werewolves left. No more howling like motivational sleepers. Now, I've got perfect ear canals. Hey, I love those bearings, where did you get yours?

It's nothing serious, but ever since I fell out of that airplane, I've been so worried about my sleeping sickness, I've got insomnia. You know how I take my privacy seriously. That's why I like to eat in the dark, even when the lights are on. Why interact with myself, if I can avoid it? In fact, whenever I drive out to Loch Ness Lake, I stay in the passing lane for as long as I can. No, I have no idea why they call it a *monster truck*. Maybe it's because of the scales? Alibi? Sure, it's got to be around here, somewhere. My late father used to say you should always tell the truth, even when you lie. Of course, I don't want to take all of the credit, so I wake up each morning, one day closer to death. Say, what have you got in your rucksack, Billy?

Obedience

It's such a chore being one of the beautiful people.

My meteorologist tells me that I should be more careful during the summer months. I wouldn't want to be kidnapped by vacationing Vikings. Yesterday, after the fumes blew in and the ants marched out, I felt feverish as a stick man at a bonfire. Everyone loves flambé, although none more than Satan.

Last night, following her brawl with the police, Cookie said, *No use crying over spilled blood, Eddie.* I'm no Jr. Mountie, but I wouldn't want to get on that horse, backward. Sure, I like calisthenics, but there's never enough hugs and kisses to go around.

After the letter bomb got lost in the mail, two suspects fled on foot. Uncle Kirby used to say, *You don't scratch, if it doesn't itch.* Of course, when it comes to 1st degree murder, there's no such thing as being too careful. Me; I do whatever I'm told.

That's Just the Kind of Guy I Am

I'm reading my mind. Hope nothing bad happens. Tammie says I'm clairvoyant, but I'm tired of talking about things before they happen. Yesterday, I spent the day sport honking in traffic and avoiding the cops. I was surprised how easy it was.

After I sell off my ammo collection, I'm going to retire early, so I can churn out a couple of country hits, and never have to answer the phone again. Fortunately for my doctor, my blood is brightest in the dark. He said if I want to see blood, I don't need to cut myself.

Last week, Tammy warned me about the 4th dimension. She said, even if I'm living in a parallel universe, it's hard to know what it's parallel to. That's probably why I can't remember things. At least I can walk on my hands. I make it look romantic. It's a gift. By the way, I'm pretty sure I was nowhere near that shooting at the mall. The newspaper said it all happened so fast.

THE DIFFICULTY OF
HISTORICAL KNOWLEDGE

Trying to avoid the annual cannibal blood drive, so I'm headed back East for a bit of seasonal left-wing leaf wrestling. Mr. Bubbles claims I have the lengthiest personality he's ever seen, but I beg to differ. After my most recent bout of amnesia, I've found my voice and bid *sayonara* to identity theft.

Last week aunt Penny sold her entire collection of two-tone antique cats and gimcrack party baubles. She's dedicating the remainder of her life to clinging to the planet. Not to mention feeding children to the wolves. Driving across this great country of ours, witnessing its recklessly deployed beauty, it's hard to know with any certainty what early humans really thought about the future. Of course, this year, for daylight saving time, we've turned the clocks back a century. Now, it's darn near impossible.

Pet Sounds

The pet snack industry is family friendly, because people are like their pets, only more so. Of course, the public is legally entitled to know what it's up against—you know, the raw, but cooked; the medium, but rare; the treble, not the bass.

Once, I took a speed sleeping course, so now I'm able to catnap in half the time. Productivity has skyrocketed. Last night, after the quarterly regional sales managers' meeting, I drove sleepily home through the night's smooth and furry dark. The streets lay down flat as an omelet and my mind wandered toward the meaning of pets. Of course, nothing good can happen when a human thinks too long about a cat. As I pulled into our driveway, I didn't hear a thing, until Mona ran out, screaming and sobbing *Tiger, Tiger*, at the top of her lungs, frantically pointing under my wheels, and offering to cut my hair for free with her newly stropped butcher knife. *Wait a minute. Who's running this meeting?* I meowed.

SINK OR SWIM

At the office, last week, without a warning, they gave me truth serum. Now, it seems everywhere I go: Styrofoam. Every damn thing floats, even my arms and legs. I can't tell if I'm hard wired or battery powered? It's like a light-headed riot. Even the astronauts are partying.

Yesterday, I took off my shoes and threw them into the pool, Sophia said it's my own fault. She said I need more promptitude, that I should comb my hair and stop looking so giddy, or else everything I say might be used against me. Of course, everyone looks guilty by 5:00 PM. For example, snakes are some of the most secretive vertebrates out there. They're not stealthy predators, they're just looking for a meal. Eat or be eaten. Like my daddy used to say about the kids on our block, *No use building a fence around it. If it's a pool, sooner or later, somebody's bound to drown.*

HALF IS BETTER THAN NONE

Thought I was taking it to the next level, until I got side-tracked on my dry-run to *Liquorland*. Must have been something in the water. They say bald men grow the thickest beards, but that's due to sin of wages. I've got three-and-a-half part-time jobs, so I ought to know. Luckily for me, I'm at one with the universe. Or two—although I hate to be duplicitous. I don't know why they don't do something about this awful weather. The flooding happens so fast, it's like nobody's business. I'd like to opt out before it does some serious damage in real time, or the other kind. Over the weekend, a few sporadic attacks were reported, but no large-scale mayhem. Apparently, the Murder-Suicide pact prevented an outbreak of total war. In fact, when I ran into Murphy at Gino's on Armistice Day, he told me he's still awaiting trial. The repeat offender charges were dropped because the prosecution couldn't locate the bodies of both the drowned twins. When I asked Murphy if he was innocent, he cracked half a smile and said, *Mostly*.

Burning Wire

No witnesses, nor any known motives, the initial police report said, although he couldn't have known that at the time. He drove 5 MPH above the maximum speed limit—hoping to put as much distance as possible between the crime scene and his still bloody hands, without attracting the attention of the highway patrol. Eventually, he knew, the police would find him, not because they were smart, but because their forensic technology was even better than their interstate communications. The broken, driver's-side window was open an inch at the top, and the wind howled like a siren. Ahead, the sun shone blood-bright as the electrical scent of burning wire rose under the hood, snaked through the firewall, and filled the car like gas fills a chamber.

COMPANY CAFETERIA

I'm lining up on both sides, just to be fair. Have you tried that new cat pizza yet? It's delicious, if you give it a chance. Of course, I have false memories from my years in beauty school, but I'm sure it's filled with vitamins and minerals. All food should be shiny and portable, like a new car. The kitchen's mostly automated, so you don't have to give the germs a second thought. Jell-O tuxedo parfait or Octopus ice cream?

Yesterday, I was feeling a little agitated because of that escaped Python in Shipping & Receiving. No, I don't remember a thing, but my supervisor tells me I grabbed it by the throat and showed it what it means to be a proud combat veteran. Who said the purpose of a bayonet is to bring a gun to a knife fight? I'm confident that the concealed weapons charges won't get in the way of the company thank-you party. My attorney has been reinstated, so I don't anticipate any glitches. Say, if you're not going to finish that, would you mind passing it over here?

Smitten

Just for a lark, I voted against myself. Yes, it hurt my feelings, but I don't like to awaken before I go to sleep. Some people think it was because of those slippery eels, but I'm in favor of all the things those naysayers are against. It's part of my wellness journey. Yesterday, while loading my double-barreled questions, I discovered, at 40, everyone gets the face I deserve. Now, no one is returning my calls. I think there might even be a little money in it.

What self-respecting taxidermist is going to stuff all those crying animals? Meanwhile, I'm channeling the ambient positivity. Like incompetence, or an all-you-can-eat buffet, it's remorseless. In fact, last night, just as I was about to wrestle that slimy gator into smiling submission, Nadine leaned close to me and tantalizingly whispered, *Did you buy me that flood insurance I've always wanted, Ralph?* So much love.

It Adds Up

While power napping in my automatic hammock, I nearly wrecked my gizmo. No, I have no idea why they call it a *monkey wrench*. I guess, these days, everything is learn-by-doing. The main problem is I'm no longer a member of my inner circle. Like a hangman's knot, I'm out of the loop. It scares my wife and nearly turned the robots into vegetarians. (Don't be fooled by the meat-eating thought bubbles.) Normally, I'm not just a short story of myself, I'm an epic. But ever since the tectonic crime wave and those carnivorous millipedes, I can barely locate my fingers— even after going to great lengths. In fact, since the most recent round of their heinous acts, the think tanks have joined forces with the willfully ignorant. Together, they've launched a rebranding campaign in support of suspicious thinking and malicious whistling, although they claim they are just helping young people study the inhumanities. Is this something anyone can do? I wish I had the answers. A hamburger here, a hamburger there; pretty soon it begins to add up. It's about time, don't you think?

CLIMATE CHANGE

It's not hard to get lost in the Insomnia islands. Everything is on fire there, as usual, although sometimes, I wish I was left-handed, so I could make some new mistakes. Sherry says, I shouldn't make any hasty judgements. Her eyes are the color of pale blue veins, her hair as beautiful as a snake's.

At the *Come-on-Inn*, an unruly customer refused to leave at closing time. Upon the arrival of the local constabulary, a number of patrons complained of his aimless bouncing and archaic dancing. *It was untimely*, one angry customer fumed. *It provoked anachronistic weeping*, another added. You might be surprised to learn just how many industrial secrets are stolen annually. Many claim it's merely innocent shoplifting, others say it's better if we keep our mouths shut.

Some days, the hot days are colder than the cold days and the cold days are warmer than the hot days, although I prefer no weather of any kind. I think we may all be owed an apology. Of course, it's not redaction, if it's merely crossed out. Yesterday, as I was practicing my cinematic technique, the room grew darker than a night flight to Guantanamo. Sherry said, *Don't you think you should get some sleep, Aron?* I reminded her, *The ocean is on death row, the continents burn like pyromaniacal Boy Scouts, and almost anything might happen, next.* I just wanted to check with her. Make sure she felt comfortable with it.

LEFTOVERS

Dancing affects some parts of the brain more than others. Fortunately, lobotomies aren't as popular as they used to be. Aren't you tired of all these counterfeit bees? All buzz, no sting. They should be kept in solitary confinement. At least it's not contagious.

Biggby is the luckiest guy I know. I'll bet he's counting his calories all the way to the bank. Not me. I'm as lucky as a four-legged spider, although no matter what you eat, you stay dead for a long time. Some say that's the secret to success. Once, I gave blood, but 25% of the population has used a firearm within the last year. It depends on your comfort-level.

Remember, multitasking isn't as good for you as originally thought, which is why I gave up humblebragging in my athleisure wear. Believe me, Valentine was no saint, even if he wore his heart on his sleeve. For better or for worse, half of all marriages end in open heart surgery. Before I dropped out, I took a class on it in med school. Naturally, it takes longer to cook a meal than to eat it. Could you hand me that scalpel, please? There might even be a little left over for you.

Variety

Yesterday, it was beautiful money weather, so I went outside and gave a green crewcut to our charismatic lawn. I used the acoustic mower because its kinder to the invertebrates. Animal misbehavior is none of my business, but at those tiny latitudes, who can blame them? Big things come in small packages.

Lately, I've been giving some thought to the crux of the matter. It's easier to lose weight than it is to get taller, but is nothing sacred? Since the onslaught of unfettered laissez-faire market discipline, my clothes have sent silent signals to the fashion enemy, so they always know exactly where to find me. Inexplicably, there have been no recent suicides in my neighborhood. Some blame it on a run of good luck, others say it's because of the preemptive euthanasia. All over the world people want something different, but to be perfectly honest, I want the same thing, a thousand different ways.

Cautious Optimist

A chain is only as strong as its weirdest kink, but it's that time of year again, when the days are getting longer and shorter. Of course, you can't blame them for trying. Not all of them are criminals.

I love candy; the more confusing, the better. In this cartoon weather, with its cotton floss clouds and nights darker than a snake slithering in mud, why wait to eat?

Say, why are there no species with three legs? Yesterday, after shopping for getaway cars, I was virtue signaling from the left-hand lane. They say that if you don't do it, it's your own fault. I think there maybe something still living inside me. Marcella says, that in order to find out, I should be drawn and quartered— in eighths. I guess a knife can be a kind of blunt instrument even if it's sharp. Just because there are no outstanding warrants for my arrest doesn't mean I can always expect things to turn out for the best.

STOLEN BIKINIS

Last night, I dreamed of lawyers. Hey, I don't make the laws. Now, I'm eating a little packet of space food and wondering, *Do flowers like sex?*

Experts say it will only get worse. When I told my shoplifter cousin, Nadine—you know, the one with that ugly bump on her head— that she might go to hell for all the bikinis she's stolen, she said, *It's not about the clothes, Clarence, it's about the weather.* Like Schrödinger's dog, I ran away.

Winter Apple Tree

Today, I'm in the vicinity of my atoms. It's not as bad as it looks. Every man is an island. Luckily, I've got my snorkel with me. On the other hand, every monologue takes two, because it takes one to know one.

Bring me a gurney, please, just to be on the safe side. These wounds are more beautiful than they look, far better than the real thing. My robot stunt double says that after the factory recall, he started to dream of blood.

My bed sleeps like a winter apple tree, silent, white, and soft.

It's lonely on the farm.

You learn something every day.

A Blast

Yesterday, on Green St., I saw an ambulance parked outside the funeral home. Picking up or dropping off? Sometimes it's hard to tell the journey from the destination. Everybody needs to live two lives at once, even if they're downsizing. I have the damndest time trying to remember my neighbors' dreams. You know how it is. Of course, it doesn't matter, when there's nobody at home.

Who says a dynamite tree doesn't know how to have a good time? Don't let the exploding fruit fool you. I was just in the Midwest with my other wife trying to square the crop circles.

It's always fun to celebrate Cowboy and Indian summer, although the best thing about Nebraska is that it's easier there to receive the secret transmissions. A lot easier than Kansas. Naturally, beggars can't be choosers, but I don't understand why my brother refuses to leave his screaming kids with me for the weekend. Nothing says *family* like the 4th of July. If only those little monsters wouldn't snuff out the glittering fuse, I know they'd have a blast.

Finishing School

Each time I weigh myself, I'm upscale. In this one house town, there's no place like home, so I'm making some lifestyle changes. For example, I'm smiling at my TV until it turns itself off. I'm taking on-line, alphabetical tap dance lessons. Someday, I'd like to sit down and have a good, long, cry, but until then, I'll be donating my body to science. Certainly, it's prudent to plan your funeral in advance, or if you can't get a head start, afterward. It's never too soon to bury the dead. Yesterday, with my eyes closed, I cut my own hair. It's not as hard as it looks, although now I understand why the Aztecs practiced human sacrifice. Here at Miss Ester's fully accredited finishing school, every day begins with a new start, although no matter how hard you try, you're never finished.

LONG BLACK CAR

This time of year, the words on everyone's lips are, *No, no, not now.* Speaking of the dead; they come from a long, venerable line. But who's counting? Not even the mathematicians. A similar method is used in slaughterhouses. I'll spare you the details. My advice to you, *Stay focused.* One size fits all. Although many quantum theorists say we should abandon any notion of cause and effect, nothing succeeds like success. Discreetly, I whisper to Mr. Ruby, *Pull up the hearse.* And wouldn't you know it? Just like that.

About the Author

Brad Rose was born and raised in Los Angeles, and lives in Boston. In addition to *No. Wait. I Can Explain.*, he is the author of three collections of poetry and flash fiction, *Pink X-Ray*, *de/tonations*, and *Momentary Turbulence*. A new book of prose poems, *WordinEdgeWise* is forthcoming.

Six times nominated for a Pushcart Prize, and three times nominated for the *Best of the Net Anthology*, Brad's poetry and fiction have appeared in over 100 journals, including *The Los Angeles Times, The American Journal of Poetry, New York Quarterly, Puerto del Sol, Clockhouse, Cloudbank, Baltimore Review, 45th Parallel, Best Microfiction 2019, Lunch Ticket*, and *Cultural Daily*. Brad is also the author of seven poetry chapbooks, including the recently released *Collateral*, and *Funny You Should Ask*.

His website is: www.bradrosepoetry.com

112 Harvard Ave #65
Claremont, CA 91711 USA

pelekinesis@gmail.com
www.pelekinesis.com

Pelekinesis titles are available through Small Press Distribution, Baker &
Taylor, Ingram, Gardners, and directly from the publisher's website.